OCT 1 3 2011

Super 'Wiches

by Marilyn LaPenta

Consultant:
Sharon Richter, MS, RD, CDN

BEARPORT PUBLISHING

NEW YORK, NEW YORK

Credits

All food illustrations by Kim Jones

Publisher: Kenn Goin
Senior Editor: Lisa Wiseman
Creative Director: Spencer Brinker
Design: Debrah Kaiser

Library of Congress Cataloging-in-Publication Data

LaPenta, Marilyn.
  Super 'wiches / by Marilyn LaPenta ; consultant, Sharon Richter.
    p. cm. — (Yummy tummy recipes)
  Includes bibliographical references and index.
  ISBN-13: 978-1-61772-306-3 (library binding)
  ISBN-10: 1-61772-306-1 (library binding)
  1. Sandwiches—Juvenile literature. 2. Cookbooks—Juvenile literature. I. Title. II. Title: Super sandwiches.
  TX818.L28 2012
  641.8'4—dc23

                             2011017967

For more information, write to Bearport Publishing Company, Inc., 45 West 21st Street, Suite 3B, New York,
New York 10010. Printed in the United States of America in North Mankato, Minnesota.

073011
042711CGE

10 9 8 7 6 5 4 3 2 1

Contents

Making Delicious 'Wiches

Use the recipes in this book to make some of the yummiest sandwiches you'll ever put in your tummy! The tasty treats in *Super 'Wiches* are easy to make. If you cut them into fun shapes, using cookie cutters or a knife, lunchtime becomes art time!

The great thing about making your own food is that you know exactly what goes into it. When you make your own sandwiches, for example, you can choose the kind of bread (whole grain is healthiest) and what goes between the slices. You can limit foods with **preservatives**, which aren't always good for you. You can also choose low-fat cheese, lean cuts of meat, and extra vegetables to make every sandwich healthier. Too many **calories**, especially from high-fat, highly **processed** foods, may lead to **obesity**. Use the ideas on page 22 for making the healthy sandwiches in this cookbook even more nutritious.

Getting Started

Use these cooking and safety tips, as well as the guide to kitchen tools, to make the best tasting sandwiches you've ever eaten.

Tips

Here are a few tips to get your cooking off to a great start.

- Quickly check out the Prep Time, Tools, and Servings information at the top of each recipe. It will tell you how long the recipe takes to prepare, the tools you'll need, and the number of people the recipe serves.

- Once you pick a recipe, set out the tools and ingredients that you will need on your worktable.

- Before and after cooking, wash your hands well with warm soapy water to kill any germs.

- Wash all fruits and vegetables that have edible skins before using them in the sandwiches.

- Put on an apron or a smock to protect your clothes.

- Roll up long shirtsleeves to keep them clean.

- Tie back or cover long hair to keep it out of the food.

- *Very important*: Keep the adults happy by cleaning up the kitchen when you've finished cooking.

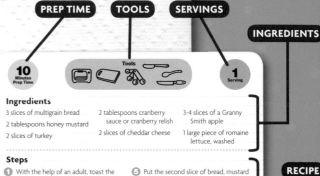

PREP TIME · **TOOLS** · **SERVINGS** · **INGREDIENTS** · **RECIPE**

10 Minutes Prep Time

Tools

1 Serving

Ingredients

3 slices of multigrain bread

2 tablespoons honey mustard

2 slices of turkey

2 tablespoons cranberry sauce or cranberry relish

2 slices of cheddar cheese

3-4 slices of a Granny Smith apple

1 large piece of romaine lettuce, washed

Steps

1. With the help of an adult, toast the bread in a toaster oven.

2. Take the bread out of the toaster oven (Be careful! The slices will be very hot.) and place it on the cutting board. With the butter knife, spread the honey mustard on one side of each slice of bread.

3. On one slice of bread, place the turkey.

4. Gently spread the cranberry sauce or relish on top of the turkey with the back of a spoon.

5. Put the second slice of bread, mustard side up, on top of the cranberry sauce.

6. On this slice, place the cheese and then the apple slices. Cover the apple with the piece of lettuce.

7. Place the last slice of bread on top, mustard side down.

8. With the help of an adult, cut the sandwich in half with the serrated knife.

There are 7,500 kinds of apples grown around the world. About 2,500 kinds are grown in the United States.

Be Safe

Cook safely by having an adult around to help with these activities:

- Using a sharp knife or peeler

- Using the stove, microwave, blender, or other electrical appliances

- Removing hot pans from the oven (*Always* use pot holders.)

- Frying foods on top of the stove (Keep the heat as low as possible to avoid burns from oil splatter.)

Tools You Need

Each recipe in this book requires a few of the kitchen tools shown below.

Spoon

Butter knife

Fork

Sharp knife

Peeler

Mixing Spoon

Sandwich cutters or cookie cutters

Potato masher

Strainer

Spatula

Measuring spoons

Measuring cups

Pot holders

Microwavable plate

Frying pan

Roasting pan

Plate

Toothpick

Drinking glass

Small bowl

Paper towels

Cutting board

Food processor or blender

Microwave

Toaster oven

Oven Stove top

Oven

Thanksgiving Treat

10 Minutes Prep Time

Tools

1 Serving

Ingredients

2 slices of your favorite bread (whole wheat or multigrain)

1 tablespoon mayonnaise

2–3 bread-size slices of turkey

¼ cup whole-berry cranberry sauce (You can use jellied cranberry sauce if you prefer.)

¼ cup **stuffing**

1 piece of lettuce, washed

Steps

1. With an adult's help, toast the bread in the toaster oven until it's light brown.

2. Carefully remove the hot bread from the toaster oven and place the slices side by side on the plate.

3. Spread mayonnaise on each piece of toast with the knife.

4. Place the turkey on top of the mayonnaise on one piece of toast.

5. Scoop the cranberry sauce onto the turkey with the spoon. Then, using the back of the spoon, gently spread the sauce.

6. Scoop the stuffing onto the cranberry sauce. If you want, warm the stuffing in the microwave, in a **microwavable** dish, for about 20 seconds before adding to the sandwich.

7. Add the piece of lettuce and then place the other piece of toast on top, mayonnaise side down.

Health Tip

White turkey meat is low in fat and high in **protein**.

Turkeys were first raised for food by Native Americans as early as 1000 AD.

Pumpernickel Veggie Delight

10 Minutes Prep Time*

Tools

1 Serving

*Plus 30 minutes roasting time

Ingredients

1 eggplant, washed (Portabella mushrooms also work great, or you can use another vegetable of your choice.)

A drizzle of olive oil

2 slices of pumpernickel bread (or your favorite whole grain bread)

1 large piece of romaine lettuce, washed

2 slices of mozzarella cheese

¼ cup sun-dried tomatoes

2 teaspoons balsamic dressing

Health Tip

Eggplant is a good source of **fiber** and is almost fat free. Like all food from plants, it has no **cholesterol**.

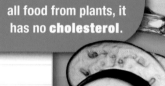

Steps

1. Preheat the oven to 400°F.

2. Ask an adult to use the sharp knife to cut off the end of the eggplant that has the stem. Then use the peeler to peel the rest of the eggplant.

3. Thinly slice the eggplant on the cutting board.

4. Spread the slices on a roasting pan and drizzle olive oil on top.

5. **Roast** in the oven at 400°F for 15 minutes. Then turn the slices over with a fork and roast for another 15 minutes. Carefully remove the pan from the oven with the pot holders.

6. Remove the excess oil on the eggplant by patting the slices with a paper towel.

7. Place a piece of bread on the plate and top it with the lettuce.

8. Cover the lettuce with about 3–4 slices of eggplant. You can use the leftover eggplant to make another sandwich, or you can store it in the refrigerator, in a plastic bag or container, to use in another meal.

9. Put the mozzarella cheese on top of the eggplant.

10. Add the sun-dried tomatoes on top and drizzle the **dressing** over the sandwich.

11. Place the other slice of bread on top and, with the help of an adult, slice the sandwich diagonally with the knife.

While many people think eggplant is a vegetable, it is actually a fruit.

Cucumber Garden Sandwich

10 Minutes Prep Time

Tools

1 Serving

Ingredients

2 large strawberries, washed

2 ounces of softened cream cheese

A **dash** of lemon juice

*Optional: ½ teaspoon **chopped** mint

2 slices of multigrain bread

6–8 thin slices of a medium-size cucumber, washed and peeled

1 tablespoon alfalfa sprouts, washed

Steps

1. Remove the stems and leaves from the strawberries. Then ask an adult to use the knife to chop up one strawberry into small pieces on the cutting board. Cut the other strawberry into slices.

2. Set aside the strawberry slices. **Mash** the chopped strawberry in a small bowl with the potato masher.

3. Add the cream cheese and lemon juice to the bowl. Continue mashing until the ingredients are well mixed.

4. If you decide to use the mint, stir it in with a mixing spoon.

5. Place the bread on the cutting board. Use the butter knife to spread the mashed strawberry mixture on each slice.

6. Arrange the sliced cucumbers and strawberries any way you want on one slice of the bread.

7. Use a knife to trim off the white stems on the alfalfa sprouts. Sprinkle the sprouts on top of the cucumbers and strawberries.

8. Put the other slice of bread on top. Cut the sandwich into triangles.

The expression "cool as a cucumber" comes from the fact that cucumbers are 95 percent water and have a cool, refreshing taste.

Turkey and Apple Stack

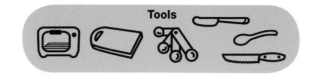

10 Minutes Prep Time

Tools

1 Serving

Ingredients

3 slices of multigrain bread

2 tablespoons honey mustard

2 slices of turkey

2 tablespoons cranberry sauce or cranberry relish

2 slices of cheddar cheese

3–4 slices of a Granny Smith apple, washed

1 large piece of romaine lettuce, washed

Steps

1. With the help of an adult, toast the bread in a toaster oven.

2. Carefully take the hot bread out of the toaster oven and place the slices on the cutting board. With the butter knife, spread the honey mustard on one side of each slice of bread.

3. Place the turkey on top of the mustard on one slice of toast.

4. Gently spread the cranberry sauce or relish on top of the turkey with the back of a spoon.

5. Put the second slice of bread, mustard side up, on top of the cranberry sauce.

6. On this slice, place the cheese and then the apple slices. Cover the apple with the piece of lettuce.

7. Place the last slice of bread on top, mustard side down.

8. Cut the sandwich in half with the sharp knife.

There are 7,500 kinds of apples grown around the world. About 2,500 kinds are grown in the United States.

Peanut Butter Creations

5 Minutes Prep Time

Tools

1 Serving

Ingredients

2 slices of your favorite bread (whole wheat or multigrain)

2 tablespoons of peanut butter

Your favorite peanut butter toppings, such as ¼ apple (washed and sliced), ½ banana (peeled and sliced), ½ pear (washed and sliced), 1 to 2 tablespoons honey, agave, hummus, jelly, or jam

Steps

1. Put both slices of bread on the cutting board.

2. With the knife, spread the peanut butter on each slice.

3. On one slice, add as many toppings as you want on top of the peanut butter.

4. Cover the sandwich with the other slice of bread.

5. Press a sandwich or cookie cutter into the sandwich to create a fun shape.

When making a PB and J sandwich, 96 percent of people put the peanut butter on before the jelly.

If you don't have a sandwich or cookie cutter, make your own! Just follow these easy steps.

1 Trace or draw the shape you want on a stiff piece of paper.

2 Cut out the shape with scissors.

3 Place the shape on top of the bread.

4 With the help of an adult, use a knife to carefully cut around the shape.

Sandwich Monsters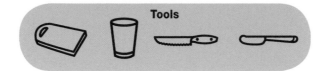

10 Minutes Prep Time

Tools

1 Serving

Health Tip

Carrots are a great source of **vitamin A**, which helps promote good vision.

Ingredients

2 slices of whole wheat bread

2 slices of sandwich meat of your choice (You can use lean turkey, ham, or roast beef.)

1 slice of cheese of your choice (Use your favorite.)

1 to 2 tablespoons of your favorite spread (For example, you can use mustard, mayonnaise, oil and vinegar, horseradish, and so on.)

A handful of decorative items to make a monster face (You can use alfalfa sprouts; blueberries; carrot slices or slivers; cucumber, olive, pickle, and radish slices; dried cranberries; raisins; roasted peppers or pepper strips. Wash these items as needed.)

Steps

1. To make the monster head, place a piece of bread on the cutting board. Turn the glass upside down and press it down on top of the bread. With help from an adult, use the sharp knife to cut around the glass to make a circle. Repeat this step with the other piece of bread.

2. Put the meat on one of the bread rounds. Trim or fold it to fit.

3. Place a slice of cheese on the cutting board. Use the sharp knife to cut one edge of the cheese into a zigzag pattern for the monster's teeth. Put the cheese on the bread so that the "teeth" extend over the edge.

4. With the butter knife, spread the mayo, mustard, oil, or any other spread you choose on top of the cheese.

5. Top the sandwich with the other bread round.

6. To finish the monster's face, add eyes (carrot slices?), a nose (a raisin or two?), and hair (alfalfa sprouts!). Use your imagination.

There are about 30,000 different types of wheat. In the United States, it's grown in 42 states.

Grilled Cheese Surprise

5 Minutes Prep Time

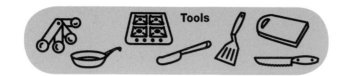

Tools

1 Serving

Ingredients

2 tablespoons butter

2 slices of whole wheat bread

2 slices of cheese (Use your favorite or mix and match.)

Surprise filling (for example, 1 tablespoon of tuna salad, a slice of ham, a piece of tomato, or a pickle slice)

Health Tip

Cheese is high in **calcium**, which is necessary for strong bones.

Steps

1. With the help of an adult, put 1 tablespoon of butter in the frying pan and melt it over low heat on the stovetop.

2. Using the butter knife, spread the other tablespoon of butter on one side of each slice of bread.

3. Put one slice of bread, butter side down, in the warm frying pan on top of the melted butter.

4. Top the bread with one slice of cheese.

5. Put the surprise filling in the center of the cheese.

6. Top the surprise filling with the other slice of cheese and then cover with the other slice of bread, buttered side up.

7. Press down on the sandwich with the spatula while it cooks.

8. After 2 minutes, slightly lift the sandwich with the spatula to see if it has browned.

9. When it has browned to your liking, flip it over to the other side. Press it down with the spatula.

10. After another 2 minutes, check the underside of the sandwich. When it is light brown and the cheese has melted nicely, move the sandwich to the cutting board with the spatula.

11. Cut the sandwich in half to see the surprise in the middle.

A person who sells cheese in a store is called a cheese monger.

Chicken-Orange Wrap

15 Minutes Prep Time

Tools
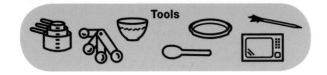

1 Serving

Ingredients

½ cup cooked chicken, cubed

¼ cup mandarin oranges, drained and cut in half

2 tablespoons dried cranberries

2 tablespoons chopped pecans

1 tablespoon honey mustard

1 8-inch whole wheat wrap or tortilla

1 large leaf of romaine lettuce, washed

Steps

1 In a small bowl, mix the chicken, oranges, cranberries, pecans, and mustard with the spoon.

2 If you want, place the wrap on a **microwavable** plate and warm it in the microwave for 35 to 45 seconds. Once you take the wrap out of the microwave, place the lettuce on top of it.

3 Put the chicken mixture in the middle of the lettuce and spread gently with the spoon.

4 Fold the left and right edges of the wrap toward the center. Then, starting with the edge closest to you, roll up the wrap and keep it together with a toothpick.

Birds are the closest living relatives to the *T. rex*, which died out more than 60 million years ago.

Health Tip

Chicken is an excellent source of **protein**. Eat it in its healthiest form by removing the skin, which is high in **saturated fat**.

Tuna-Avocado Roll-Up

 10 Minutes Prep Time

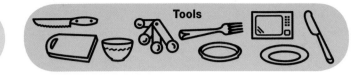 Tools

1 Serving

Ingredients

1 ripe avocado

2 teaspoons lemon juice

White tuna packed in water, either 1 pouch or ½ of a 7-ounce can, drained

¼ cup celery, washed and diced

1 scallion, washed and cut up

1 tablespoon Dijon mustard

1 2-ounce flax roll-up (about 9 x 7 inches) or a wrap of your choice

½ tomato, washed and diced

Steps

1. Ask an adult to cut the avocado in half on the cutting board and remove the pit. Then, use a fork or spoon to scrape the flesh out of the skin into the bowl.

2. Add the lemon juice to the bowl. Then mash the avocado with the fork.

3. Add the drained tuna, celery, scallion, and mustard. Mix well with the fork.

4. If you want, warm the roll-up in the microwave, on a **microwavable** plate, for 35 to 45 seconds. Once you take the roll-up out of the microwave, place it on a cutting board.

5. Spread the avocado mixture on the roll-up with the butter knife, leaving a 1-inch space around the edge.

6. Sprinkle the diced tomato on top.

7. Tightly roll up the sandwich, put it on a plate, and cut it in half.

Health Tip

One-fourth of a medium avocado has only 80 calories and nearly 20 **vitamins** and minerals.

Hundreds of years ago, some people called the avocado an "alligator pear," because the fruit's rough skin resembles an alligator's skin.

17

Breakfast Egg Wrap

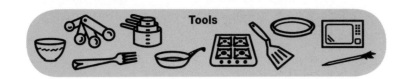

10 Minutes Prep Time

Tools

1 Serving

Ingredients

2 eggs

1 tablespoon milk

¼ cup shredded cheese (Use your favorite kind.)

¼ cup cooked ham or turkey, cut into small pieces

2 chopped scallions, washed and chopped

A dash of salt and pepper to taste

1 tablespoon butter

1 whole wheat wrap or tortilla (8 inches)

*Optional: ketchup

Steps

1. Crack both eggs on the side of the small bowl and let them slide in. Add the milk and **whisk** together with a fork.

2. Stir in the cheese, ham or turkey, scallions, and salt and pepper. Then put the bowl to the side.

3. Put butter in a frying pan. With help from an adult, melt it over low heat on the stove top.

4. Pour in the egg mixture. Stir frequently with the spatula until the eggs are cooked to your liking.

5. If you want, place the wrap or tortilla on a **microwavable** plate. Warm it in the microwave oven for 35 to 45 seconds. Use the spatula to scoop the eggs into the middle of the warm wrap.

6. Fold the left and right edges of the wrap toward the center. Then, starting with the edge of the wrap closest to you, roll it up. Use a toothpick to hold the wrap together.

7. If you like, dip the sandwich in ketchup as you eat it.

Health Tip

Egg yolks are one of the few foods that naturally contain **vitamin D**.

White-shelled eggs are produced by hens with white feathers and white earlobes. Brown-shelled eggs are made by hens with red feathers and red earlobes.

Black-Bean Spread with Salsa

20 Minutes Prep Time

Tools
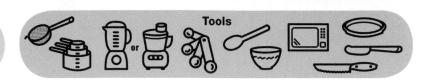

1 Serving

Health Tip

Black beans are filling, full of **fiber** and **protein**, and very inexpensive.

Ingredients

1 15-ounce can of cooked black beans

¼ cup olive oil

1 tablespoon lemon or lime juice

1 teaspoon garlic powder

A pinch of salt and pepper

1 roll-up (about 9 x 7 inches)

2–3 slices of cheddar cheese

¼ cup salsa

¼ cup sliced avocado

5–6 slices of red onion

*Optional: ¼ cup sliced black olives

Steps

1. Pour the beans into a strainer and rinse them with cold water.

2. With the help of an adult, put the beans into a food processor or a blender with a drop of olive oil and pulse for 20 seconds. Then turn the food processor or blender on to run continuously, carefully drizzling in the rest of the olive oil and the lemon or lime juice until the bean mixture is fairly smooth. This should take about 1 minute.

3. Use the spoon to scrape the bean mixture into the bowl. Then stir in the garlic powder and salt and pepper.

4. If you want, put the roll-up on a **microwavable** plate. Then warm it in the microwave for 35 to 45 seconds.

5. Carefully take the plate out of the microwave. Use the butter knife to spread the black bean mixture on the roll-up, leaving a 1-inch space on all four sides. Put aside any leftover bean mixture for later use.

6. On top of the bean mixture, layer the cheese, salsa, avocado, onion slices, and olives, if desired.

7. Carefully roll up the wrap and cut it into thirds.

This bean spread may also be used as a dip with chips or vegetables. It can be stored in a sealed container in the refrigerator for two to three days.

Salad Medley

10 Minutes Prep Time

Tools

1 Serving

Ingredients

1½ cups assorted raw vegetables, washed (Choose at least 4 of your favorites.)

2 tablespoons of your favorite **dressing**

1 whole wheat pita

1 to 2 romaine lettuce leaves, washed

Steps

1. With the help of an adult, cut the vegetables into bite-size pieces on the cutting board.

2. Place the vegetables in the bowl, and pour the dressing over them. Mix with the spoon until the vegetables are coated.

3. Cut the pita in half. Then open the pocket in each half. Place the halves on a plate.

4. Rip the lettuce leaves into pieces, dividing them equally to fit in the 2 pita pockets.

5. Spoon half the vegetables into one of the pita halves and then fill the other half with the remaining vegetables.

6. Enjoy your sandwich salad!

Health Tip

Romaine lettuce has more **vitamins**, such as **vitamin C**, than many other types of lettuce.

The "pocket" in pita bread is created by steam as the bread cooks. The steam puffs up the dough. As the bread cools and flattens, a pocket is left in the middle.

Chicken and Grapes with Yogurt Dressing

 15 Minutes Prep Time

Tools

 1 Serving

Plus 30 minutes to chill, if desired

Ingredients

¼ cup plain yogurt

1 teaspoon honey

1 teaspoon Dijon mustard

¼ cup cooked chicken, cut into bite-size pieces

6–8 seedless grapes, washed and cut in half

¼ cup diced celery, washed

¼ cup chopped walnuts

A pinch of salt and pepper

1 pita

1 lettuce leaf, washed

Steps

1. Put the yogurt, honey, and mustard in a bowl. Stir well with the mixing spoon to **combine** the ingredients so they make a dressing.

2. Put the cut-up chicken into the other bowl. Add the halved grapes, celery, and walnuts. Mix with the mixing spoon.

3. Add the salt and pepper.

4. Pour the yogurt **dressing** on the chicken mixture and mix well.

5. If desired, chill the chicken in the refrigerator for at least 30 minutes.

6. With the help of an adult, use the knife to cut the pita in half on the cutting board.

7. Put a lettuce piece in each pita pocket and scoop in the chicken with a spoon.

8. Place the sandwich on a plate and enjoy!

Health Tip

Yogurt is a good source of **calcium** and **protein**. It helps bones stay strong.

One grapevine can grow up to 50 feet long and have about 40 **clusters** of grapes. There are about 75 grapes in a cluster.

Healthy Tips

Nutrition Facts
Serving Size ... (200g)
Amount Per Serving
Calories 150   Calories from Fat 35
% Daily Value*
Total Fat 4g
 Sat. Fat 3g
 Trans Fat 0g
Cholesterol 10mg
Sodium 65mg
Total Carbohydrate 8g
 Fiber 0g
 Sugars 8g
Protein 20g   40%

Vitamin A 2% • Vitamin C 0% • Calcium 20% • Iron 0%

*Percent Daily Values (DV) are based on a 2,000 calorie diet

Always Read Labels

Labels on packaging tell how many **calories** are in each serving of a food and how many servings are in a package. They also have information about fat, sugar, **vitamins**, and other **nutrients**. Too many high-calorie foods in a person's diet can lead to weight gain and other problems over time, especially when those calories mainly come from fat and sugar.

Make Recipe Substitutions

While all the recipes in this book call for wholesome ingredients, you can often reduce the calories and get rid of **unhealthy fats** by substituting one ingredient for another. For example:

Bread
Use bread, pitas, and wraps that are 100 percent whole wheat or 100 percent whole grain. They are usually low in fat and have lots of **fiber**, vitamins, minerals, and **antioxidants**. Eating whole grains can help protect a person from heart disease, strokes, diabetes, and **obesity**.

Dairy
Mayonnaise: Use low-fat mayonnaise.

Cheese: Try low-fat cheeses.

Cream cheese: Use low-fat cream cheese or Neufchâtel cheese, which is lower in fat than regular cream cheese.

Yogurt: Use fat-free or low-fat yogurt instead of full-fat yogurt.

Milk: Use low-fat or skim milk instead of whole milk.

Meat
Use lean meats such as turkey. To avoid **preservatives**, use fresh meat.

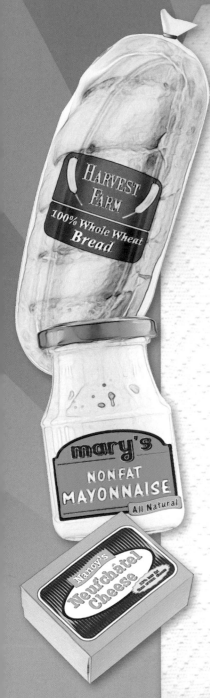

Glossary

antioxidants (*an*-tee-OK-suh-duhnts) substances found in certain foods that may prevent cell damage, which can cause disease in people and animals

calcium (KAL-see-uhm) a chemical found mainly in bones and teeth

calories (KAL-uh-reez) measurements of the amount of energy that food gives you

cholesterol (kuh-LESS-tuh-rol) a fatty substance people need to digest food; too much in the blood can increase the chance of heart disease

chopped (CHOPT) cut into little pieces

clusters (KLUHSS-turz) bunches, a number of things of the same kind held together

combine (kuhm-BINE) to join together

dash (DASH) a small amount of something

dressing (DRESS-ing) a sauce or other liquid topping for a salad

fiber (FYE-bur) a substance found in parts of plants that when eaten passes through the body but is not completely digested; it helps food move through one's intestines

mash (MASH) to crush or pound into a soft mixture

microwavable (*mye*-kroh-WAYV-uh-buhl) safe to use inside a microwave oven

nutrients (NOO-tree-uhnts) proteins, vitamins, and other things in food that are needed by people to stay healthy

obesity (oh-BEESS-uh-tee) a condition in which a person is extremely overweight

preservatives (pri-ZUR-vuh-tivz) things, such as chemicals, used to keep food from spoiling

processed (PRAH-sesst) food that has been altered from its natural state with preservatives, flavor enhancers, coloring, and other additives

protein (PROH-teen) a substance found in all living plants and animals; essential for growth and for the repair of tissues

roast (ROHST) to cook in a hot oven

saturated fat (SACH-uh-*ray*-tid FAT) unhealthy fat found in butter, whole milk, and high-fat meats that can raise a person's cholesterol levels, increasing the risk of heart disease

stuffing (STUHF-ing) a mixture of breadcrumbs and other chopped foods used to stuff meats such as chicken

unhealthy fats (uhn-HEL-thee FATS) fats that are not good for a person's health

vitamin A (VYE-tuh-min AY) a type of vitamin found in sweet potatoes, spinach, peaches, and other foods; helps improve and preserve eyesight

vitamin C (VYE-tuh-min SEE) a type of vitamin found in fruits and vegetables; it's important for healing the body and keeping teeth and bones strong

vitamin D (VYE-tuh-min DEE) a type of vitamin found in milk, cheese, butter, and a few other foods; it helps promote strong bones

vitamins (VYE-tuh-minz) substances in food that are necessary for good health

whisk (WISK) to mix something very quickly

23

Index

Bibliography

D'Amico, Joan, and Karen Eich Drummond. *The Healthy Body Cookbook.* New York: John Wiley (1999).

Dobrin, Arnold. *Peter Rabbit's Natural Foods Cookbook.* New York: F. Warne (1977).

Read More

Lobb, Janice. *Munch! Crunch! What's for Lunch? (At Home with Science).* New York: Kingfisher (2000).

Wolf, Laurie Goldrich. *The Do It Myself Kids' Cookbook.* New York: Downtown Bookworks (2010).

Learn More Online

To learn more about making super 'wiches, visit
www.bearportpublishing.com/YummyTummyRecipes

About the Author

Marilyn LaPenta has been a teacher for more than 25 years and has published numerous works for teachers and students. She has always enjoyed cooking with her students, her three children, and her three grandchildren. Marilyn lives in Brightwaters, New York, with her husband, Philip.